WELCOME
TO THE
FAMILY

WELCOME
TO THE
FAMILY

MEMORIES *of the* PAST

for a BRIGHT FUTURE

Marlene Kim Connor

Broadway Books

New York

Broadway Books titles may be purchased for business or promotional use or for special sales. For information, please write to: Special Markets Department, Random House, Inc., 1745 Broadway, New York, NY 10019.

PRINTED IN THE UNITED STATES OF AMERICA

BROADWAY BOOKS and its logo, a letter B bisected on the diagonal, are trademarks of Random House, Inc.

Visit our Web site at www.broadwaybooks.com

First edition published 2006

Book design by Michael Collica

ISBN 0-7679-2193-3

1   3   5   7   9   10   8   6   4   2

To Reggie, Max, John, Clifton, Kelvin

Mom (1921–1985)

Dad (1923–1999)

And my sis, Debbie

Family is forever.

CONTENTS

Welcome to the Family 1

PART ONE

People You Need to Know About: Great-Grands,

Grandparents, and All Kinds of Grand Folks 3

PART TWO

About the One You Love 43

PART THREE

In the Kitchen 77

PART FOUR

Important Things I Came to Know About

Your Beloved, About Life 89

Acknowledgments 97

To

_____

From

_____

WELCOME TO THE FAMILY

Memories of the Past for a Bright Future

What a wonderful time this is. Both of our families are growing. We've all imagined this time would come one day, and it's so exciting.

Families are often little units. People joined together, growing up together, creating a quilt of experiences. When the new person enters, there can be so much we all want to share, to say, to remember, and sometimes to suggest.

From this day forward our lives will intersect. With this gift of memories from the past, I hope to help make your future together as smooth and as happy as it can possibly be.

There will always be bumps along the way—glorious, rewarding, challenging bumps. They are the stuff of life, of love, and of marriage. This collection of moments from the past may help. Maybe an insight into the one you love will be the key one day, or perhaps the key will be as simple as a favorite bowl of soup. You'll know.

Here's a little gift to help and support you throughout this adventure. And to welcome you to the family.

PART ONE

People You Need to Know About:
Great-Grands, Grandparents, and
All Kinds of Grand Folks

Family means more than a mother, father, and children. A true family encompasses a spectrum of people—those we love, those who have loved and cared for us, and those who share our laughter and our sorrow. Family members are the people who shape our lives.

OUR FAMILY TREE

Your New Spouse/Birthday/Birth Order

Sibling/Birthday/Birth Order

Spouse/Birthday

Child/Birthday

Child/Birthday

Sibling/Birthday/Birth Order

Spouse/Birthday

Child/Birthday

Child/Birthday

Sibling/Birthday/Birth Order

Spouse/Birthday

Child/Birthday

Child/Birthday

Sibling/Birthday/Birth Order

Spouse/Birthday

Child/Birthday

Child/Birthday

Mom/Birthday

Dad/Birthday

My Mother/Birthday

My Father/Birthday

Dad's Mother/Birthday

Dad's Father/Birthday

MY FAMILY

You may want to know what sort of people they were.

A LITTLE ABOUT MY MOTHER

Country/city of origin: _____

Did my mother's family have an "old country"? _____

_____

_____

Where my mother was raised: _____

Faith: _____

_____

Politics: _____

_____

Career/work: _____

_____

_____

A LITTLE ABOUT MY FATHER

Country/city of origin: _____

Did my father's family have an "old country"? _____

_____

_____

Where my father was raised: _____

Faith: _____

_____

Politics:_____

_____

Career/work:_____

_____

What I remember or know about my grandparents:_____

_____

_____

_____

_____

_____

_____

I always chuckle when I recall:_____

_____

_____

_____

_____

_____

DAD'S FAMILY

You may want to know what sort of people they were.

A LITTLE ABOUT DAD'S MOTHER

Country/city of origin:_____

Did his mother's family have an "old country"?_____

_____

_____

Where his mother was raised:_____

Faith:_____

_____

Politics: _____

_____

Career/work: _____

_____

A LITTLE ABOUT DAD'S FATHER

Country/city of origin: _____

Did his father's family have an "old country"? _____

_____

_____

Where his father was raised: _____

Faith: _____

_____

Politics:

Career/work:

What we remember or know about Dad's grandparents:

Dad always chuckles when he recalls:

What really stuck from our family legacies:

Important family members who died before our children really
knew them:

 MOM & DAD

No two people are alike.
How can two adults expect to blend easily?
Yet together we created a family.
Here's who we are.

Where I was born:_____

Where I was raised:_____

As a child, I was:

[ ] spunky   [ ] high-spirited

[ ] shy   [ ] athletic

[ ] dreamy   [ ] challenging

[ ] self-sufficient   [ ] intense

[ ] musical   [ ] sweet

My background could be described as:

[ ] upper class   [ ] middle class

[ ] working class   [ ] striving class

[ ] just classy   [ ] no class

Where Dad was born:_____

Where Dad was raised:_____

When Dad was a child, he was:

[ ] spunky   [ ] high-spirited

[ ] shy   [ ] athletic

[ ] dreamy   [ ] challenging

[ ] self-sufficient   [ ] intense

[ ] musical   [ ] sweet

Dad's background could be described as:

[ ] upper class   [ ] middle class

[ ] working class   [ ] striving class

[ ] just classy   [ ] no class

Dad's work before we met:_____

_____

My work before we met:_____

_____

Where Dad and I met:_____

_____

How we met each other:_____

_____

_____

Our favorite thing to do while courting:_____

_____

Where we were married:_____

_____

Where we lived when the first baby came:_____

_____

Where we moved to:

What were those early years like?

Our family grew, our work life changed.

Dad:

Mom:

Where did we finally settle?

OUR TOWN

*I hope these memories of our earliest days as a
family will help you enjoy the moments of your
earliest days as a family.*

Why did we move there?_____

_____

_____

_____

_____

How big a town was it?_____

_____

The cultural mix:_____

_____

The neighbors:

_____

_____

_____

_____

Did we like it? Did we fit in?

_____

_____

_____

_____

Our town could boast that:

_____

_____

_____

_____

_____

MARRIAGE

Our journey may help you in your journey.

The early years: _____

_____

_____

_____

The middle years: _____

_____

_____

The long haul: _____

_____

_____

_____

Did we honor traditional gender roles (Mom raised the kids, Dad was the provider), or were the lines blurred (Mom in the board-room, Dad in the kitchen)?

_____

_____

_____

_____

_____

The roller coaster of marriage was up when:_____

_____

_____

_____

_____

_____

The roller coaster of marriage was down when:_____

_____

_____

_____

ABOUT ME

For better or worse, here's who I think
I am. Some of these traits were bound to rub
off on those I raised.

I absolutely avoid:_____

_____

I have faith in:_____

_____

I have faith that:_____

_____

I enjoy a good:_____

_____

I would best describe myself as (introvert? extrovert? bold? moody?):

_____

_____

Some of my favorite things:_____

_____

_____

_____

_____

Some things I hate, but change is always possible:_____

_____

_____

_____

I always wanted to:_____

_____

_____

_____

_____

What impresses me

   In people: _____

   In the world: _____

   In the home: _____

What does not impress me: _____

_____

_____

_____

You may notice that I'm always the one who: _____

_____

_____

_____

_____

My role model was (I looked up to): _____

_____

_____

_____

_____

I mentored:_____

_____

_____

_____

My mentor was:_____

_____

_____

_____

I search my soul

    [ ] always   [ ] often

    [ ] occasionally   [ ] never

Okay, here's the great debate in a nutshell: I think people are most defined by:

    [ ] nature (genes)   [ ] nurture (environment)

    [ ] definitely a combo   [ ] never really thought about it

❊ ABOUT DAD ❊

Some dads are the force, some are the enforcer, some are comforting, some are never comfortable. Here's a glimpse of Dad, in all his glory.

Dad would absolutely avoid:_____

_____

Dad has faith in:_____

_____

Dad has faith that:_____

_____

Dad enjoys a good:_____

_____

Dad would describe himself as (introvert? extrovert? bold? moody?):

_____

_____

Some of Dad's favorite things: _____

_____

_____

_____

Some things Dad hates, but change is always possible: _____

_____

_____

_____

Dad communicates best by: _____

_____

_____

The kids consider Dad to be: _____

_____

_____

Dad sees your beloved as:

Your beloved sees Dad as:

The relationship between your beloved and Dad could be described as:

Okay, here's the great debate in a nutshell: Dad thinks people are most defined by

[ ] nature (genes)   [ ] nurture (environment)

[ ] definitely a combo   [ ] never really thought about it

DIGGING DEEP

Here's that word: Perfect. No one is perfect, though some come close. It's time to 'fess up and admit we've got quirks, ways, styles, attitudes—dare we say, eccentricities?

Okay, I'm not perfect. Here's what others accuse me of, and what I'll admit to:_____

_____

_____

_____

Lord knows Dad's not perfect. Here are quirky ways of Dad's that you should know about:_____

_____

_____

_____

Though I suspect this will be left blank, here's what Dad sees as my quirky ways:_____

_____

_____

_____

_____

Things I'm proud I accomplished:_____

_____

_____

_____

_____

_____

Things Dad is proud he accomplished:_____

_____

_____

_____

_____

_____

Siblings: Your beloved's siblings are not perfect either. Nothing to worry about, but here are some traits:

Name_____

_____

_____

Name_____

_____

_____

Name_____

_____

_____

Name_____

_____

_____

Name_____

_____

_____

THE FAMILY DYNAMIC

As we mature and blend, members of the family often develop a style that contributes enormously to the family unit. No matter how vital, no matter how strange, none of these traits is carved in stone because we all grow and change.

In our family these people played these particular roles:

The ally: _____

The mentor: _____

The go-between: _____

The peacemaker: _____

The comic relief: _____

The optimist: _____

The realist: _____

The shoulder: _____

PARENTING STYLE

Sometimes a couple's differences become tricky
when baby makes three (or more).

Which of us was the "final word"? How did the kids know

this was it?_____

_____

_____

Uh-oh, time for disciplining. Whose job was it? What did we do?

_____

_____

Were we strict or liberal?_____

_____

_____

Was our home quiet or chaotic?

Were we messy or neat freaks?

Money and kids: Do they go together?

Did we assign privileges and chores?

Was there payment for chores?

Were there gender-based chores?

Who handled homework?

OUR FAMILY MISSION,
❊ OR WHAT THE NEIGHBORS ❊
DON'T KNOW ABOUT US

Some families are held together with glue, some with cement. Some are defined by where they come from, some by where they're headed. Most of us never think about having a definition, but when asked we often realize, "Yes, my family focused on music, or business, or sports, or education, or faith." Others may answer, "My family is defined by our history, or by striving to be American." There are families dedicated to keeping their eyes on the prize. Our family, like most, had a texture all its own.

Defining our family mission:_____

_____

_____

_____

What "family" means to us:

Our family motto:

Books and music we shared as a family, or what I tried my best to
expose my children to:

Movies we enjoyed as a family:

Favorite television programs throughout the years:

_____

_____

_____

_____

My memories of family vacations, road trips, camping, and travel, and why they stood out for me: _____

_____

_____

_____

Here's how the family celebrated birthdays: _____

_____

_____

_____

_____

Important family holidays and how we celebrated them:

Holiday:_____

How we celebrated:_____

_____

_____

Holiday:_____

How we celebrated:_____

_____

_____

Holiday:_____

How we celebrated:_____

_____

_____

What about parties? Were we party-goers or party-givers?_____

_____

_____

Old skeletons that never should have been hidden?_____

_____

_____

A HOUSE IS A HOME

Under every roof is a story: unique people with
special talents and everyday faults.

Siblings, rivalries, and partnerships:_____

_____

_____

_____

_____

_____

I could expect help:

    [ ] in the kitchen   [ ] around the house

    [ ] around the yard   [ ] with the groceries

    [ ] when company came   [ ] with the accounting

Privacy issues (of course, this needs to stay just between us):

_____

_____

_____

_____

_____

_____

_____

Some children just _know_ or can sense things. One knows what makes Dad "tick." Another knows what to say to calm the waters at a given time. Here's what I think your beloved really knows:_____

_____

_____

_____

_____

_____

_____

_____

_____

THE VILLAGE

Raising a family is rarely done alone. There are relatives,
teachers, neighbors, friends, and confidants who share time,
wisdom, energy, and talents. They are forever in our hearts.

The Godparents and why we chose them:_____

_____

_____

_____

_____

I'd like to tell you about the relatives who proved invaluable, and
the folks who proved to be better than blood to our family:

    Name:_____

    _____

Name:

Name:

Name:

Folks on the invitation list whom you may not know but who are so, so important:

Name:

Name:

Name:

Name:

Name:

Name:

PART TWO

About the One You Love

It's hard to believe the day has come when our baby is getting married. It all went too quickly. Yet there were days when time seemed to stand still. The house was a wreck, there was homework to get done, and the dishes were still on the table. We couldn't wait for the kids to grow up!

Our memories return to us like waves. We watch our grown-up son fiddle with a cuff link and we remember the first day he actually cared about which pair of pants to wear. We see our daughter writing in a day planner and we remember the first time she mapped out her own book report. Our memories seem to be more than just special moments; they feel to us like signs of the future. Our children's habits, milestones, the things they cherished, all seem to hold meaning about their future selves.

These memories might one day hold less meaning because your time together will mold your beloved into a new person, into your partner. You will learn about each other in your own way and in your own time.

GROWING UP TOGETHER

*Sample these thoughts at your will. Time makes
them fuzzy; love makes them glow.*

A few things I treasure about your beloved:_____

_____

_____

A few things that drove me up a wall:_____

_____

Neatnik or slob?_____

_____

Organized? Chaotic?_____

_____

Funny little habits worth noting:_____

_____

_____

Favorite family pets:_____

_____

_____

Wild animals your beloved forced upon us, or we had to hear about

incessantly, including creepy crawly things:_____

_____

Sports played or watched like crazy?_____

_____

As a youngster there were some budding talents:

[ ] Drawing   [ ] Singing

[ ] Dancing   [ ] Performing arts

[ ] Painting   [ ] Sculpting or pottery

[ ] Decorating   [ ] Other talent

[ ] Comedy   _____

I fear that this particular hidden talent still needs to be explored:

_____

_____

Chess, Legos, sewing, any special skills that surprised us: _____

_____

_____

As a youngster these were the favorite books, stories, fairy tales: ____

_____

_____

As a teen these books, stories, stars, movies, TV shows, and plays
became a passion:_____

_____

_____

Superheroes or superstars we had to live with or, better yet, playing
"dress-up" in front of the mirror:_____

_____

_____

Must-have presents through the years

The "Santa" years:_____

The middle years:_____

The prom years:_____

The college years:_____

Morning rituals through the years:_____

_____

_____

_____

Bedtime rituals through the years:_____

_____

_____

_____

Smitten for the first time:

Who was it?_____

How did it go?_____

_____

_____

TEMPERAMENT

Some children are simply always pleasant. Some never smile.
As they get older, they become someone you don't even know.
Be forewarned!

Up and down? Sunny and bright? Sullen and difficult? Spirited?
Moods by the calendar? _____

_____

_____

_____

_____

After a busy or stressful day, we could expect: _____

_____

_____

_____

Right after school a young child's temperament can truly be revealed. Some children need to be alone. Some need to talk. Still others need to cuddle and feel reassured.

After school your beloved: _____

_____

_____

As a youngster was your beloved affectionate, a cuddle-bug, a hugger, a smoocher, aloof, reserved, or cautious? _____

_____

_____

Luck. Some are gifted with luck; others create their own opportunities:

    [ ] Lucky   [ ] Unlucky

    [ ] Created their own luck

A fear was conquered when: _____

_____

_____

What we could expect if anger flared:

[ ] a quiet storm   [ ] tears

[ ] things thrown   [ ] shouting matches

[ ] doors slammed   [ ] World War III

[ ] a combo platter   [ ] no expression

[ ] other (this needs explanation!)

_____

_____

I see my influence when:_____

_____

_____

_____

_____

I see Dad's influence when:_____

_____

_____

_____

_____

_____

Has your beloved been:

    [ ] self-analytical   [ ] self-assured

    [ ] self-indulgent   [ ] altruistic

    [ ] a bit of a bully   [ ] bullied a bit

    [ ] cliquish   [ ] gossipy

    [ ] a worrier   [ ] a free spirit

Self-reliance came one day when:_____

_____

_____

That ego! We had to bump it up or tone it down:_____

_____

_____

Introvert or extrovert?_____

_____

_____

Partier or homebody (or something in between)?_____

_____

"Most popular" or content with a close friend or two (or something in between)? _____

_____

_____

_____

_____

Competitive or laid back? _____

_____

Aggressive or passive? _____

_____

Every child has a style for trying to get what he or she wants—whether it's a toy, an outfit, some cash, or the car. Your beloved's way of getting what he or she wanted was: _____

_____

_____

_____

_____

Okay, let's say there was a real conflict. The animal instincts had to take over. Which was it, fight or flight? _____

_____

How did your beloved handle:

The word "no"? _____

_____

Being sick? _____

_____

Transitions? _____

_____

Change? _____

_____

Losing? _____

_____

Winning? _____

_____

Criticism? _____

_____

Reversals (disappointments)? _____

_____

THOUGHTFULNESS

There are moments when your child does something, shares something, or says something truly special, and wants nothing in return. Miracles do happen!

Moments of kindness:_____

_____

_____

_____

_____

Presents I cherished:_____

_____

_____

_____

_____

A special moment between us that only I remember: _____

_____

_____

_____

_____

_____

A moment when I knew adulthood was on the horizon: _____

_____

_____

_____

_____

That kid really made me feel proud when: _____

_____

_____

_____

_____

GOOD LOOKS AND BRAVADO

Everyone has at least some vanity.

Was the mirror a friend or a foe?

Grooming took this long:

Styles that mattered:

An attitude or phase that took hold:

GOALS AND DREAMS

Through marriage you'll come to know what was once
important to your beloved. These are some accomplishments
that I remember really made a difference.

What became important over the years:
_____
_____
_____
_____
_____

What dreams were realized:
_____
_____
_____
_____

What dreams were given up: _____

_____

_____

_____

_____

_____

_____

_____

_____

What dreams may be yet to come: _____

_____

_____

_____

_____

_____

_____

_____

_____

❊ SCHOOL ❊

Let's face it, school is half our childhood.

Which school was the favorite? _____
_____
_____
_____
_____

Favorite subject: _____
_____
_____

Favorite teachers: _____
_____
_____

Extracurricular passions: _____
_____
_____
_____
_____

So no one is forgotten, here are the school chums through the years
whom I remember most: _____
_____
_____
_____
_____
_____

School milestones (Spelling success at last! Sportsmanship finally
developed!): _____
_____
_____
_____
_____
_____

Always good at:

Never quite good at:

Was learning a passion or a struggle?

A MIND THAT WASN'T WASTED

For many kids, one day the brain kicks in
and opinions begin to form.

Causes that became a passion: _____
_____
_____

Politics began to creep in: _____
_____
_____

We finally agreed that: _____
_____
_____

But we never did agree about: _____

_____

_____

Your beloved was:

    [ ] a furious debater   [ ] stubborn and unyielding

    [ ] manipulative   [ ] a reasonable compromiser

    [ ] something in between

THE REAL DEAL

Time to get real about the one you love: everyone
has a dark side. Are you prepared?

Oops, you married a nut. Here are some quirks that just wouldn't go
away: _____

_____

_____

Someone your beloved never liked: _____

_____

Something your beloved never liked: _____

_____

_____

A truly embarrassing moment:_____

_____

_____

_____

_____

Get ready, here's what to expect when the going gets tough:_____

_____

_____

_____

_____

Discipline, that ugly word. How did it go?_____

_____

_____

_____

"Help me." When did (does?) your beloved really need help?_____

_____

_____

_____

My secret way that seems to work sometimes. It might work for you, too: _____

_____

_____

_____

_____

_____

_____

_____

Of course, I don't really know, but here's what kind of parent I think your beloved will be: _____

_____

_____

_____

_____

_____

_____

SPIRITUALITY

Children bring purpose and focus into their parents'
lives. Suddenly everything has meaning and consequence.
Faith, beliefs, a connection to something greater than
ourselves sometimes can be the only place to turn if
things get really crazy.

Was church/temple/worship a large part of our lives?

Did your beloved enjoy going to church/temple?

Here are some friends from church/temple:

_____

_____

_____

Was your beloved comfortable with prayer/reverence?

_____

_____

_____

Would your beloved say his/her spiritual/religious experience was:

[ ] dictatorial   [ ] boring

[ ] enlightening   [ ] comical

[ ] useful   [ ] confusing

[ ] fun   [ ] infinitely valuable

[ ] fascinating   [ ] mumbo jumbo

Did any of it sink in?

_____

_____

_____

THE NAME GAME

Most parents agonize over choosing their baby's name. So maybe names are important. Nicknames come and go over the years. One child is called "Cookie" by Grandpa; another is called "June Bug" by relatives down South. "Junior" is popular when a name is shared, and "Peanut" is another popular food item–as–nickname.

Does your beloved's name have meaning or significance?

How or why did we choose it?

Here are nicknames your beloved had to endure, and why the names stuck:

❊ YOUR BELOVED AND I ❊

Here's the hard part. Your beloved and I have shared so much together. Our relationship means something to me and something different to my child. Here's a glimpse into how I feel.

I admired that: _____

_____

I was tough about: _____

_____

I was nervous when: _____

_____

I admit I resented: _____

_____

Parents think they're the ones doing the teaching. Then one day we realize we've been taught something by our child. Children definitely teach patience. They often teach us how not to argue or that we need to stop bad habits in order to be good role models.

Here is what my child taught me

About myself:_____

_____

About my life:_____

_____

About our family:_____

_____

About the world:_____

_____

About herself/himself:_____

_____

About life itself:_____

_____

One mother said thanks to her firstborn for making her a mother and then thanks to the secondborn for making them a family.

Here's what your beloved added to our family dynamic: _____

_____

_____

_____

_____

_____

_____

_____

_____

_____

_____

_____

_____

_____

_____

THE VITAL STATISTICS

Some details of your beloved as a newborn. (They may
come in handy someday if you become parents, or
you may just be curious.)

Height: _____

Weight: _____

Hair: _____

Eyes: _____

General health: _____

Early disposition: _____

Sleeping habits: _____

Special "loveys" or stuffed animals: _____

Did your beloved suck his or her thumb or have a blankie? _____

_____

PART THREE

In the Kitchen

Wouldn't eat meat. Hates bread. Loves pesto. Eggs and toast for dinner. How about the three-year-old who would only eat the salad at McDonald's! Food is a surprising source of aggravation in many a home. Still, for bringing everyone together, preparing a meal and eating together have yet to be topped.

❧ DAY-TO-DAY DINING ❧

You are how you eat.

Here are some cravings I had while carrying your beloved:

_____

_____

_____

Some families eat together at a table, sharing thoughts of the day. Others grab a meal and plop down in front of the television. Still others eat in shifts or in separate groups—Dad in the living room, Mom and the kids at the kitchen table.

Our regular meals were eaten: _____

_____

_____

Who did most of the cooking?

Who was likely to help prepare a meal?

What was Dad's favorite meal to prepare?

What was your beloved's favorite meal?

My go-to meal to prepare (or, I know *everyone* will eat this):

Foods from our heritage:_____

_____

_____

Were we a soda family or a milk family?_____

_____

Junk food or always healthy?_____

_____

Weekday breakfasts were:_____

_____

_____

Sunday breakfast was:_____

_____

What we considered to be a "snack":_____

_____

A special treat was:_____

HOLIDAY MEAL MENUS

Some holidays came with the same foods every year.
Here's a typical glimpse of what we got used to.

Holiday:_____

    Menu:_____

    _____

    _____

    _____

Holiday:_____

    Menu:_____

    _____

    _____

    _____

Holiday: _____

   Menu: _____

_____

_____

_____

Holiday: _____

   Menu: _____

_____

_____

_____

Holiday: _____

   Menu: _____

_____

_____

_____

RECIPES TO MAKE YOUR JOURNEY EASIER

Here's the stuff your beloved loves! You will create your own family cuisine over time, but there's nothing wrong with being ahead of the game with some of our family favorites. Sometimes a familiar meal can go a long way toward soothing, bonding, curing, and comforting the savage beasts within all of us. Familiar foods from childhood bring joy and memories, even when they tasted none too good (and no one let on)!

My recipe for: _____

_____

_____

_____

_____

_____

My recipe for: _____

_____

_____

_____

_____

_____

_____

_____

_____

My recipe for: _____

_____

_____

_____

_____

_____

_____

_____

_____

My recipe for:

My recipe for:

My recipe for:_____

_____

_____

_____

_____

_____

_____

_____

_____

_____

My recipe for:_____

_____

_____

_____

_____

_____

_____

_____

_____

_____

_____

My recipe for: _____

_____

_____

_____

_____

_____

_____

_____

_____

_____

My recipe for: _____

_____

_____

_____

_____

_____

_____

_____

_____

_____

PART FOUR

Important Things I Came to Know About
Your Beloved, About Life

Here's a place for me to pour out complicated and wonderful feelings. Maybe it's a chance to get misty.

Here are my reflections, my wisdoms, and my unique memories. Here is my advice, my favorite sayings. Here's my place to reveal, my place to store truisms. Here's my place to just talk and talk and talk, without restraint, without shyness, without repercussion.

No one knows everything, no one knows if they're right about anything. But as someone once shouted to his friend when his friend questioned something he'd said, "Look, I'm telling you what I *know!*" Enjoy, and take it for what it's worth.

❈ ACKNOWLEDGMENTS ❈

I'd like to thank the ladies of Wednesday night for listening. I'd really like to thank my agent, Liza Dawson, and the very cool Trish Medved, Beth Datlowe, and the Broadway Books team. It's been a pleasure.

Thanks to the Lynches and Glomstads.

Finally, I'd especially like to thank my village: Rhonda, Marlene, Tenzin, Sossia, Edie, Marc, Cheryl, Lucia, Pat, Ralph and the folks at the Southdale YMCA, and those at Cornelia Elementary School, especially John Etnier (an awesome principal), and Katy and Ralph Campbell.

Thanks all.

ABOUT THE AUTHOR

Marlene Kim Connor, author of *What Is Cool? Understanding Black Manhood in America*, is a literary agent and the mother of two boys.